Text by: Didier Pou
Photographs: APA-POUX Co

SARLAT
AND THE PERIGORD NOIR

AS DE COEUR COLLECTION
Post card Editions
APA-POUX. L.T.D. ALBI (France)

Practical information Sarlat

- **Tourist office:** Place de la Liberté, B.P. 114, 24200 Sarlat. Phone: 53.59.27.67.
- **Museum of Sacred Art:** (Chapelle des Pénitents Blancs): Open from Easter to 15th October.
- **Museum aquarium:** Open from 15th June to 15th September from 10 a.m. to 7 p.m. The rest of the year from 10 a.m. to 12 p.m. and 2 p.m. to 6 p.m.

- **Sarlat Theatre festival:** July-August. Festival office: Hôtel Plamon, 24200 Sarlat. Phone: 53.31.10.83.
- **Music festival:** During the entire holiday season.

(Photo Studio Tourny)

An evening during the Theatre Festival on the market square in front of Chassaing residence

The castle circuit

Fenelon castle:
Open all year. Phone: 53.29.84.04 or 53.29.81.45. In summer from 9 a.m. to 12 p.m. & 2 p.m. to 7 p.m. In the off season from 9 a.m. to 12 p.m. & 2 p.m. to 6 p.m.

Veyrignac castle:
Open all year from 10 a.m. to 12 p.m. and 2 p.m. to 7 p.m. Phone: 53.28.13.56. Off season for groups, reservation.

Castelnaud castle:
Open from 12/4 to 20/4 - From 1/5 to 15/11 - From 25/12 to 3/01. From 1/7 to 31/08, 10 a.m. to 7 p.m. every day. Out of season from 10.30 a.m. to 6.30 p.m. Closed on Saturday and Monday.

Milandes castle:
Open from Palm Sunday to 15/10 and from 1/07 to 31/08, 10 a.m. to 11.30 a.m. and 2 p.m. to 6 p.m.

every day. Out of season from 10.30 a.m. to 11.30 a.m. and from 2.30 p.m. to 6.30 p.m. every day. Phone: 53.29.50.73.

Beynac castle:
Open from 1/04 to 15/11. High season from 1/04 to 30/09 from 10 a.m. to 12 p.m. and 2.30 p.m. to 6.30 p.m. Low season from 10 a.m. to 12 p.m. and 2.30 p.m. to 6 p.m. Phone: 53.29.50.40.

Grotte de la Hall (caves) Domme:
Open from 1/04 to 31/10 from 8 a.m. to 12 p.m. and 2 p.m. to 7 p.m. Out of season on appointment at the Tourist Office. Phone: 53.28.37.09.

Puymartin castle:
Open from 1/05 to 30/09 from 10 a.m. to 12 p.m. and 2 p.m. to 6.30 p.m. Out of season on request and for groups, minimum 30 persons. Phone: 53.59.29.97.

Périgord recipes

■ *Walnut cake*:

**Preparation 20 mins, baking time 45 mins.
3 eggs, 250 gms sugar, 125 gms butter + 20
gms for the cake tin, 25 cls milk, 250 gms
flour + 10 gms for the cake tin.
100 gms walnut kernels, 12 kernels for deco-
ration, 1 packet of yeast, 2 packets of vanilla sugar.**

Cream the butter, incorporate the sugar and
the egg yolks one by one, add the flour and
yeast (or baking soda) the milk, vanilla sugar.
Mix well.
Incorporate the beaten egg whites lightly and
the roughly chopped walnuts.
Pour into a greased and floured cake tin,
cook in a moderate oven 45 minutes.
Decorate with the remaining walnuts.

■ *Foie gras souffle*:

**Preparation 20 mins, cooking time 25 mins.
300 gms "foie gras", 3 eggs, 30 cls fresh
cream, 30 gms butter, salt, pepper.**

Push the foie gras through a sieve and mix
lightly with the egg yolks and cream. Season
with salt and pepper.
Add the stiffly beaten egg whites.
Put into a greased souffle mould.
Cook 25 minutes, in a hot oven (thermostat
7, 220° c)

Bon appetit!!!

A bouquet of Perigord "cepes"

PREFACE

It is rare to find so many sites of natural beauty and such a profusion of interesting places as in the Périgord Noir. Each year, an increasing number of tourists visit this region bathed by the peaceful waters of the Dordogne.

The Dordogne castles display their riches in the soft, pastoral surroundings. All is harmonious, the buildings with their regional architecture blend pleasantly into the surrounding countryside of wooded hills and majestic valleys. The small valley of Vézère hidden in the depths of craggy cliffs reveals its ancestral souvenirs of the prehistoric men who lived in the area.

Since the Cro-magnon era, generations of men have followed in succession, conserving their heritage, their traditions and life's pleasures.

Today, the people of the region are delighted to welcome you and share the "treasures" of Périgord Noir.

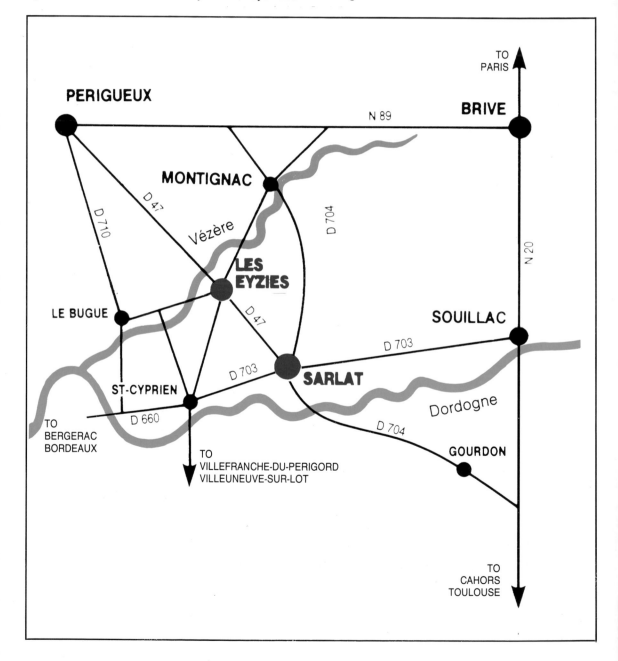

At present, the Périgord region comprises the department of Dordogne. It is the third largest French department in the area, and features a diversity of scenery spead over several small regions: to the North-East, Périgord Vert, lower down, Périgord Blanc and central Périgord, to the South-East, Périgord Noir. The latter is bordered by two winding rivers: the Vézère and the Dordogne which meet at Limeuil, forming two majestic meanders (Panat and Tremolat).

A region of light-coloured limestone, Périgord Noir takes its name from the dark forests of chestnut trees, of green oaks and pines which cover the land.

Eugene le Roy, the famous author of "Jacquou le Croquant" has one of his heros say "There are woods and woods, and little dells with murky fields... It's wild and dark. Sometimes, you can walk for half an hour or an hour without sighting a house, and when you are in its depths, in the woods, you could cry for help and no-one would hear".

In this region of forests and caves, SARLAT, the capital sprang up on a small stream, the Cuze. With its stone and slate-tiled roofs, the city was made a diocese and was the seat of a seneschal until the Revolution. Today, Sarlat is the sub-prefecture of the Dordogne with about 11 000 inhabitants. For many years, tourism has been increasing and the town is also economically favoured by a well-developed stock-feed industry, tobacco factories and surgical material production.

Finally, we must remember that Périgord Noir is a region where "gourmets"can enjoy a rich and varied selection of specialties. This is the land of the truffle, named in the area "the black diamond", of cepes (mushrooms) which proliferate the forests, geese, ducks and the famous "foie gras". The regional recipes have been passed down from generation to generation and delight the finest palates with their succulent savours. The "tables gourmandes", the name given to restaurants serving food of an excellent quality, are plentiful and your stopovers can be highlighted by the best dishes a region can offer.

Have a happy stay in Perigord Noir!

Aerial view of Sarlat

Republique Street, also called "La Traverse", which crosses the town from north to south. We can still see some of the old ramparts which surround the city in front of which there are now peripheral boulevards. In the foreground, Grande Rigaudié square is a green patch amongst the closely-knit buildings. Saint Sacerdos cathedral in the Eastern section and the former Saint Marie Church form the historical centre of this

(Photo Studio Tourny)

medieval city. We can distinguish several fine facades of residences or private homes in the photo, but we particularly notice the beautiful roofs of stone and slate tiles.

820-840:
Foundation of a Benedictine monastry by the monks of Calabre abbey who transported the relics of St Sacerdos (presumed bishop of Limoges).

1147:
Saint Bernard visits Sarlat and performs the famous miracle of the "loaves which cured".

12th century:
The abbey continues to prosper. The monastry is the temporal lord of the city, but conflict develops between the monks and the townspeople.

1223:
The citizens of Sarlat swear loyalty to King Louis VIII.

1229:
On signature of the Book of Peace, the townspeople acquire their political independance and can now govern themselves freely through their consuls.

13th august 1317:
Pope Jean XXII makes Sarlet a diocese; the city is growing rapidly with already 6 000 inhabitants.

Hundred years war:
The town remains loyal to the king of France and courageously resists but with the treaty of Bretigny in 1360, Jean le Bon delivers the entire Périgord region to Edward III of England.

1450-1500:
After a devastating war, a new period of prosperity begins for the town. Numerous houses and private residences are built as well as Saint Marie Church. The early 16th century is marked by many plague epidemics and famine which was rampant in 1516.

Wars of Religion:
For the first time in its history, Sarlat is taken by surprise on the 22nd February 1574 by the knight of Vivans, the Protestant leader. The town is pillaged and occupied for three months and the relics of Saint-Sacerdos are destroyed.

1557:
The Viscount of Turenne attempts to occupy the town but despite 6 000 troops, Sarlat resists the protestant assault which was to raise the siege.

Late 16th, early 17th century:
The Croquant revolt, a Périgord peasant movement, shakes the region but has very little effect on Sarlat.

1652:
"La Fronde" was the last important historical event in the city. Marsin, the lieutenant of Condé, took Sarlat by siege and pillaged it during a period of three months.

Life in Sarlat became more peaceful up until the Revolution during which the city remained moderate. During the Bonaparte consulate and the administrative re-organisation of the country, Sarlat lost many of its privileges. It thus became the sub-prefecture of the department. The royal court of justice was replaced by a magistrate's court, the city lost its rank of diocese and the last bishop was transferred.

FAMOUS PERSONALITIES OF SARLAT

Etienne de la Boétie (1530-1563): A brilliant jurist, he was the friend of Michel de Montaigne and the author of "La Servitude Volontaire". (Volontary Servitude).

Jean de Vienne (1557-1608): From a modest family, he became the general finance inspector under Henry IV, then president of the Audit Office.

Jean Tarde (1561-1636): Vicar general, the king's Chaplain author of several scientific works and the famous "Chronicles" of the history of Sarlat.

François de Salignac de la Mothe Fénelon (1651-1715): Born at Fénelon Castle, archbishop of Cambrai, tutor of the duke of Bourgogne, grandson of Louis XIV; renowned author of the adventures of Télémaque.

Jacques de Maleville (1741-1824): Born at Domme, lawyer at Bordeaux, writer of the Civil Code; senator and member of the Chamber of Paris.

Jean-Baptiste Sirey (1762-1845): Famous jurist. Under Jacques de Maleville's direction, drafted the famous "Recueil général des lois et arrêts" (General compilation of laws and decrees) which continued to be published after his death under the name "Recueil SIREY".

Général Compte Fournier Sarloveze (1773-1827): Empire General, he distinguished himself during the Spanish and Russian campaigns. Under the Restoration, he became general inspector of the cavalry.

Gabriel de Tarde (1843-1904): Professor at the college of France, and the author of numerous sociological studies, he was one of the founders of social and criminal psychology.

Visit of Sarlat

Sarlat, the capital of the Perigord Noir is a Middle Age city which has been remarkably conserved. Strolling through the small streets in the historical centre, you are seemingly transported centuries back into a past rich in glorious memories.

A town of merchants, clerks and men of the cloth, Sarlat developed due to its commerce and its fairs which still exist today. Far from the great economic crossroads, the city fell into slumber after the Revolution and its old quarters were thus conserved intact. With the Malraux Law of the 4th of August 1962, the restoration of the old section of the city which had become derelect was undertaken. A new life was given to the brown buildings.

We suggest a circuit which enables you to visit the buildings of essential interest. At least two hours are necessary to fully appreciate these features. If you have more time, you can discover other streets and houses full of charm and beauty.

If you have parked your car on Grande Rigaudie Square, coming from Tourny street you should arrive at Peyrou Square (Place du Peyrou). Our itinerary starts from here.

Turning your back to La Boétie résidence (which we will see again later) you will see before you:

Saint-Sacerdos cathedral

In 1317, Jean XXII, the Pope of Avignon and a native of Cahors promoted Sarlat to the rank of bishopric in an attempt to increase the authority of the church over the small town.

The abbey church built in the 12th century was no longer fit for the celebration of services. In 1231, Raymond de Roquecorn, the city's first bishop, began renovation work on the old building using a part of the diocese revenues.

The construction of the cathedral took many centuries with various difficulties due to the 100

The former cloister of Saint Sacerdos cathedral

◀
The facade of la Boétie residence coming from Tourny street

The funeral garden slopes down in terraces in front of Saint Sacerdos cathedral chevet whose enormous buttresses reinforce its facade

Years War, the religious wars, epidemics and above all, financial problems.

Finally, the Roman church was demolished on the 18th July, 1504 and on the 6th February, 1505, work began on the new building, inaugurated by the Vicar general Jean de Magnanat and Guillaume de Plamon, the chapter provost. Construction work was directed by the architect Pierre Esclach and the builder Blaise Bernard, master mason of Sarlat.

The cathedral was finally finished in the last quarter of the 17th century. The long period of construction explains its irregular aspect — a mixture of the Roman style of the former church with various additions during the 14th, 16th and 17th centuries.

The entrance in front of us is the only section remaining from the old abbey church. Apart from the entrance door, enlarged in the early 18th century, the facade is entirely Roman. The first section consists of Lombardy style bands. In the second section, semicircular arches rest on groups of columns. The third section was built later and dates from the 17th century.

At the top, a curious bulb-shaped tower topped by a small bell was built in the 18th century by Bishop Alexandre le Blanc.

The interior of the cathedral forms one vast nave without a transept. There are four bays flanked by lateral chapels on the lower sides. The choir consists of five large archways opening onto the light-filled chapels and the chevet of the former 14th century Saint-Sauveur cathedral. The vaulting was constructed between 1682 and 1685 under the episcopate of François II of Solignac de la Mothe Fénelon, and is supported by enormous cylindrical pillars

to the sacristy, the former capitularly chapel of the abbey. To the right again, slightly in front, we will take the exit door which leads us to the former monastry cloister.

On the wall, we can distinguish the position of three ribbed archways which have been filled in. To the left in a recess is **the Blue Penitents chapel** (sometimes called Saint-Benoît chapel) which was restored in the 17th century. It is composed of a single small nave lit by splayed windows and is characterised by its Roman architecture. Light floods in and enhances the

The "Lantern of the Dead" seems to watch over the city from the heights

which separate it from the lower section. Built in the spirit of the great churches of southern France, the building as a whole is impressive in its combination of majesty and simplicity.

In the lateral chapels, we note the fine furnishings, the 17th and 18th century altar-pieces, 15th century wood-work and situated between St Peter and the Guardian Angel chapel is a beautiful stone Pieta, set into a recess, dating from the 15th or 16th century. At the back of the church, we note the fine organ-case executed by Jean François Lépine in 1750.

Opposite the choir to the right, a door leads

warm colour of the stones.

The altar situated in the choir is of hewn stone and is lit from behind by two windows. From the outside, we note the unusual view of the cathedral bell-tower and the southern facade reinforced by enormous flying buttresses.

We cross over a small porch and come to the **cour des Fontaines**, (Fountain courtyard). Turning left, we head towards the **cour des Chanoines**, (Canon's courtyard) which is embellished by a fine half-timbered house with its overhanging upper storey and a 15th century house

FOURNIER SARLOVEZE

Like many Empire generals, François Fournier, born in 1773 at Sarlat in the Endrevie quarter, came from a modest family. A fervent republican, he joined the army in the Revolution and was rapidly promoted. In 1799, he became colonel of the 12th Hussards.

Forthright in character, an admirer of Bonaparte but not of Napoleon, his career followed its course according to the emperor's favour or disfavour of him. Promoted to brigade general in 1807, then division general, he took part in the Russian campaign and the famous crossing of the Beresina. Under Louis XVIII, he became inspector general of the cavalry and was made a count. Lieutenant general count Fournier-Sarlovèze died in Paris on the 17th January, 1827 and was buried at Sarlat.

The funeral path, a large burial ground, is seemingly closely linked to the Lantern of the Dead

with transom windows.

We skirt the exterior of the blue Penitents chapel along the chevet which brings us to the garden behind the cathedral, (jardin des enfeus). This was formerly a burial ground and has been transformed into terraces. The wall contains numerous funeral recesses and we can distinguish the coats of arms of former noble Sarlat families. At the top of the terraces overlooking these old tombs stands a curious tower:

The Lantern of the dead or Saint-Bernard Tower

This is a strange 12th century edifice dominating Sarlat both architecturally and by its origins which remain an enigma. It is composed of a cylindrical tower surmounted by a conical roof of crown-shaped stone tiles.

The room on the ground level was originally completely closed in by a ribbed vault whose keystone represented the Paschal lamb. It is lit by three splayed windows.

The upper floor, divided externally by a section supported by corbels (brackets) is composed of decreasing bands in the form of a pignon. The roof contains four small openings.

The tower was built after Saint-Bernard's visit to Sarlat and its original purpose remains an enigma. We know that it was consecrated as a chapel and was used as a burial place. Due to its original structure and its mysterious aura, it was used by the townspeople for the election of their consuls in the 17th century. Finally, decadance obliging, it was transformed into a powder-room after the Revolution.

We continue towards Montaigne Street (rue Montaigne), a charming typical lane from where there is a fine view of the cathedral chevet and Peyrou square (Place Peyrou). We can the take the street opposite us, (rue Sylvain Cavaillé), or descend a little further to the beginning of Albusse street. The building on our left is the former residence of the General, Count Fournier Sarlovèze.

At n° 4, above the door in a recess in the corner of the wall, we notice a statue of the Virgin. All of the houses in Sarlat feature these, as in many towns of Southern France where the Virgin Mary watches over the city. At the corner of Albusse street and the blind alley named "Impasse de la Vieille Poste", we discover the beautiful overhanging facade of a private residence. A little further along this alley, are the former Royal Post-house and the post-horse relay station.

►

A typical house in Montaigne street

*The overhanging facade
of the small blind alley
named "la Vieille Poste"*

*The 15th century entrance
door of the Grézel residence*

Continuing along Albusse street, we turn right into Landray street which leads to the entrance of the former **"Présidial"**. This was the Royal Courthouse and was restored by Henry II in 1552, abandoned in 1560, then again re-established in 1641. With the Revolution, Sarlat became a departmental sub-prefecture following reorganisation of the administrative services. From then on, only a magistrate's court remained which is now established on Grande Rigaude Square.

The "Presidial", an unusual building, is surrounded by a pleasant garden (quite rare inside the old part of the city). The facade contains two bay windows, one above the other, through which a stone staircase and a beautiful balustrade of wrought iron can be seen. On the roof of the building is a curious polygonal lantern held up by wooden props.

We now turn back towards Salamander street via Presidial street in which we admire the beautiful facades of private residences: Hotel de Genis or Beaupuy (15th century) at number 6b., a little further on, at number 1, on the edge of a small square - **Grezel residence**, the former home of a magistrate whose fine 15th century facade entrance gate decorated with a salamander, opens onto a beautiful stone staircase.

As we walk down the small street, we come to Liberty Square, formerly Royal square. On our right is the **Town Hall**.

The garden and the facade of the "Présidial", the former court-house of the city

Built in the early 17th century by an architect/mason from Montpazier, Henri Bouyssou, it stands on the site of the former "communal house". It is rather plain and austere in style. The ground floor features wide arcades while the high windows of the first storey are surmounted by a frieze of Greek motifs. On the roof an unusual bell-turret is supported by cylindrical columns.

On Saturdays, a market is held in **Liberty Square** which takes on a lively and colourful appearance. Market stalls and stands cover the entire square and local produce (ducks, geese, truffles and cepes according to season) are sold.

For the time being, we will turn our attention away from the left side of the square and head towards number 16 Fénelon street where the previous residence of the Fénélon family stands.

Opposite the Town Hall is a large building abandoned since the Revolution. It is the former **Saint-Mary's church**. Its construction was decided upon by the townspeople in 1365 and work began in 1367. Partly because of the Hundred Years War, the completed church was finally consecrated on Easter Monday of 1507 by Monseignor Gontaut-Biron. It was used as a par-ish church until the Revolution, then in 1793, it was converted into a saltpeter factory. Pillaged and mutilated, it was sold in 1796 and in 1815. The choir was then cut off from the church and today it forms the market-place where numerous plays are performed during the summer festivals.

Disfigured by the small shops surrounding it, we notice in particular, the magestic square Gothic bell-tower. Light floods in through its wide ribbed bay windows.

Rising up to the right at the top of the slope is the hexagonal tower of the **Chassaing or Gison residence**, built in the 16th century. It is a remarkably pure and sober construction, characterised by its high and rather severe facade.

We continue towards the goose market square and arrive at Consuls street. In front of us, **Selves de Plamon residence** occupies a large section of the street. It was the home of a family of drapers in the 12th century and is undoubtedly one of the finest homes in the town.

On the ground floor are two large ribbed arches. Three ribbed windows with Gothic tracery denote the importance of the Plamon family over the centuries. In 1330, Guillaum Plamon was elected consul of the city. The family

On Liberty square, Chassaing or Gisson residence (16th century)

◄

Liberty square, previously named Royal Square, the centre of the city and marketplace

The beautiful 17th century staircase
of solid wood in the Tapinois
de Bétou residence

Saint Marie fountain - a refreshing stop
for visitors in summer

The audacious squinch (horn-shaped)
at the corner of Consuls street

became richer with the honours conferred upon it and the residence was enlarged. A second storey was built with rectangular windows framing dog-head gargoyles. The entrance door is decorated with a pediment featuring the arms of the Plamon family. (Still visible). The next building is often confused with the Plamon residence and features an enormous 17th century staircase of oak and chestnut with solid wooden steps and an interior courtyard whose facade is decorated with Gothic openings.

Opposite is the small Saint-Marie fountain which flows out from under a wide broken-vaulted arch. At the corner of Consuls street opposite La Paix street, we notice a beautiful squinch which formerly housed a shoemaker's shop. It supports a terrace decorated with a wrought-iron balustrade belonging to the Bétou residence. This street contains many fine residences: At number 9 is the 15th century Vassal home, the Mirandol residence and yet others with their beautiful entrance doors.

To the right of Liberty square, returning towards the cathedral, is the tourist office housed in the fine **Vienne or Maleville residence**.

◄
The House of Consuls

*The small stream named "la Cuze"
flows under Albéric Cahuet street,
buried beneath Sarlat*

*The facade of Vienne or Maleville
residence (16th century) which
faces Liberty square.
It is now the Tourist office*

The main section of Vienne
or Maleville residence

JEAN DE VIENNE

The story of this man's life seems rather banal nowdays, however at the time, it resembled a fairytale. Jean Vienne was born at Sarlat in June 1557, of a modest family. His origins destined him to follow the normal course of a person with his background. He thus began work as a mule tender. The bishop however, was impressed by his intelligence and decided to send him to study in Bordeaux. A brilliant career thus began. He quickly became the king's secretary at the Chancellery, then General Finance Inspector and Councillor of State. He was finally named president of the Audit Office in 1601 under Henry IV. He died in 1608.

Vienne residence dates approximately from the mid-16th century and consists of several old homes made into a single dwelling.

The entrance door situated on the small square is decorated with medallions worn with time on which we can distinguish an M, the initial of the Maleville family, framing the portraits of Henry IV and Marie de Medicis or Gabriel de Estrées.

The building features a terrace above the entrance door overlooking an Italian Renaissance style facade. A small overhanging tower, the distinguishing sign of nobility, embellishes the overall structure.

The residence juts out on the right towards Liberty square and terminates in a gabled facade similar to that of Boétie residence.

Inside is a large room with a French style ceiling featuring a very beautiful fireplace with hunting motifs. (A deer lying between two dogs).

Following the small lane to the left of the courtyard, we enter a new section of the city which has been restored due to a law, (Loi Malraux), passed on the 4th August 1962. This law concerned the restoration of protected sectors of old cities. There is a succession of small streets, courtyards and arched passages in which we admire the fine half-timbered facades of former private residences. We pass through Henry de Ségogne passage, the courtyard and blind alley named "Les Violettes" arriving at Henri Malraux square, after which we return to Peyrou square. To the left is the birthplace of Etienne de La Boétie, a magnificent home which stands in front of the cathedral and the former bishop's palace.

This beautiful home in "Les Violettes" courtyard is a fine example of the restoration work done since 1962

The small passage named "Henry de Segogne" leads to André Malraux square and Peyrou square

La Boétie residence, (16th century)

Etienne de la Boétie was born in 1530 in the home built by his father, Antoine de la Boétie between 1520 and 1525.

Of Renaissance style, it features a wide rounded opening on the ground floor topped by an entabulature held by two columns on each side. On the left side of the building is an archway opening onto a vaulted passage. The facades feature beautiful transom windows framed by pilasters decorated with medallions or lozenges. The roof slopes steeply and the gable is decorated with cabbage motifs. Nowdays, the Boétie residence, one of the "jewels" of the old city, houses the Chamber of Commerce.

From 1318 to 1790, a bishop resided in Sarlat. Today, only the facade of the former bishop's palace remains adjoining the door and bell-tower of Saint-Sacerdoce cathedral. These old buildings were constructed under the Italian cardinal Nicolo Gaddi, the Bishop of Sarlat in the 16th century.

From the facade, we can admire the fine Gothic windows with their stone bars on the first

The facade of la Boétie residence (16th century)

and second floors. Above is an Italian Renaissance style gallery and the roof is supported by short cylindrical columns. The last floor is embellished by a small corner tower.

We return to Liberty square by way of Liberty street which features other beautiful facades: At number 5, La Mothe residence has a fine entrance door decorated with friezes. There is also the Pharmacy residence with its half-timbered facade and at number 9, the 16th century Dautrerie residence.

The main street built in 1837 crosses Sarlat from north to south, dividing the city in two. It is rue de la Republique (Republic street) called "La Traverse" by the citizens. It is a shopping street and leads us to **the western part of the city** - a former working-class quarter in comparison to the residential area which surrounds the cathedral.

Opposite rue des Consuls (Consuls street) we take rue des Armes (Arms Street) which features fine 15th century private residences, amongst them Ravilhon residence at n° 2 with its Gothic openings and transom windows. Crossing a porch, the street climbs up towards the former ramparts. We return towards the main street by Papucie street where we take Jean-Jacques Rousseau street. At the beginning of this street is the **Penitents Blancs Chapel** featuring a large

NICOLO GADDI

In this period, the clergy of Sarlat were no longer free to elect their bishop who was named according to the king's decision. In 1533, Queen Catherine de Medicis named her cousin and "good friend", Nicolo Gaddi, the Bishop of Sarlat. The latter was an important Florentine lord who lived in Rome. He was rarely in residence in Sarlat and his first visit to the city took place eight years after his nomination in 1541.

Interior of the Pénitents Blancs Museum, the former chapel of Récollets convent

The facade of Ravilhon residence (15th century) in les Armes street

A beautiful flower-covered home at the corner of J.J. Rousseau and La Boétie streets

Baroque door with columns topped by two beautiful scrolls. The inside of the chapel has been transformed into a museum containing remarkable objects of religious art: statues, clothes, shrines and books. There is also ancient pottery, a collection of fire-backs, old coins, maps documents and works on the Sarlat area.

A little further, at the corner of this street and La Boétie street is the **former Sisters of Saint-Clair Convent**, (17th century), of which a beautiful cloister remains. Continuing by Siège street, we notice a fine 14th century building with Gothic windows at the corner of rue de Turenne and the Cerval residence at n° 13.

Finally we descend towards the centre of the town taking Trois Conils street and Rousset street which features a round 15th century **watch-tower** with machicolations (Saint-Clair residence).

This section is undoubtedly less endowed architecturally than the centre but is nevertheless worth visiting and a stroll through its alleys can reveal many unsuspected features of interest.

Perigord Noir circuits

Dordogne Valley circuits

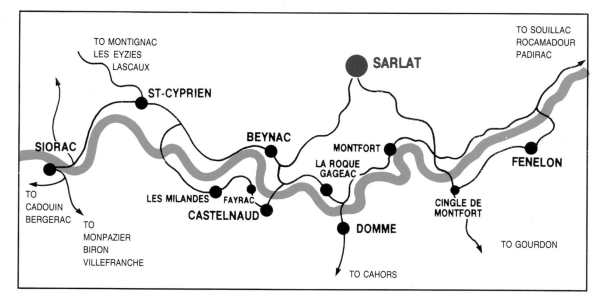

Fénelon Castle

From Sarlat, we take the road to Gourdon (D 704). Just before the small village of Grolejac, the road forks to the left and we follow the D 50 which brings us to Fénelon Castle, 6.5 kms further on.

The castle is situated on the border of the Perigord and Dordogne departments. It is a feudal fortress and was formerly the home of the Salignac-Fénelon families. The renowned Archbishop of Cambrai, tutor of the Duke of Borgogne and author of the adventures of Telemaque was born here in 1651.

The castle is open to visits and behind its ramparts there are three fortified walls and 13 watchtowers. From the highest curtains, there is a splendid view of the Dordogne valley. Inside the castle is a cloister, a court of honour, a chapel and a room in which various souvenirs of Fénelon are exhibited. The castle also contains a remarkable collection of old cars which date back to 1895.

Veyrignac Castle

A few kilometres away, **Veyrignac Castle** welcomes us. This feudal castle was the home of the Marquis de Therme. (Louis XIV's Marshal). It was burnt down by the Germans in the last war but has now been very well restored. We can visit the arms galleries and an astonishing torture chamber. Hot-air balloon flights are organised from the castle.

Montfort Castle · Cingle de Montfort

We turn towards Carcac taking the road forking left to Vitrac. (D 703). A few kilometres away on a rocky promontory stands the powerful castle of Montfort. Fief of the bloody Bernard de Casnac, it was razed by Simon de Montfort in the early 13th century. A strange malediction seemingly took hold of the castle and it was destroyed and rebuilt again three times during the 100 Years War and the wars of religion.

The present castle dates from the 15th and 16th centuries. It is privately owned and not open to visits. On the way to the castle, from a bend in the road, there is a splendid view of the **"cingle de Montfort"**, a beautiful meander formed by the Dordogne which we admire as it stretches out over the entire width of the valley.

Aerial view of Montfort Castle

Domme

We continue along the right bank of the river passing through Vitrac. We cross the Dordogne and head towards Domme. The road now climbs up above the valley.

The village of Domme was built on a "promontory hanging between the valley and the sky" on an enormous rocky "dome" at a height of 150 metres overlooking the Dordogne which meanders peacefully below.

Situated on an exceptional site, at the crossroads of main regional roads, a feudal castle marked the spot until 1280. In this year, the King of France, Philippe le Hardi had a fortified village constructed around it, asserting its strength over the wealthy lords of the area.

It was occupied by the English during the 100 Years War, then by the Hugenots under the command of the famous Protestant captain, Geoffrey de Vivans during the wars of religion.

Domme was built according to the strict architectural principles laid down for fortified cities with its streets intersecting at right-angles. Its general form is trapeze-shaped however, thus adapting to the shape of the land.

With its flower-filled lanes and its old houses of honey-coloured stones and brown tiles, the town of Domme has conserved its charm.

Inside the town, we discover numerous monuments: the city wall with its fortified doors, Tours door, in which the Templier knights were imprisoned from 1307 to 1318 (graffiti engravings inside), del Bos door and La Combe door. The town hall should be visited as well as the Governor's house (15th century), the Paul Reclus museum and the 17th century market square which contains the entrance to the magnificent caves of Domme. These feature numerous stalactites and stalagmites whose sparkling crystals can be admired. From La Bare lookout, there is a splendid panorama over the valley. The view is also impressive as we walk beneath the cliff.

We now return to the right bank of the Dordogne and head towards one of the most beautiful villages of the Perigord region.

Tours Door at Domme

The old covered market and the governor of Domme's house

Del Bos Door at Domme

La Roque-Gageac

Castelnaud castle, separated from its rival, Beynac castle, by the Dordogne

La Roque Gageac

Built against the rock-face at the foot of the cliff covered in green oaks, the houses of this small town spread out along the Dordogne river.

Its hewn stones and rocks are bathed in soft light and the exceptional beauty of its natural site cannot but enchant the visitor.

The 15th century castle of Milandes underwent extensive restoration at the beginning of the century before becoming the famous home of Josephine Baker

Josephine Baker's bedroom in which the visitor can see one of her dresses laid out on the bed

In the Middle Ages, the small town was practically impregnable, well protected behind its walls and prospered due mostly to the fishing trade.

Nowdays, the closely built houses leave just enough room for the picturesque lanes through which we climb up towards the fortified church and the Tarde family manor.

At the extremity of the village, Malartrie Castle, built in 15th century style was the home of a retired ambassador, Count St. Aulaire, the remarkable Talleyrand historian.

We continue our route along the right and left banks alternatively, arriving at the magnificent site of Castelnaud Castle

Castelnaud castle

On a rocky promontory at the confluence of the Dordogne and Cerou rivers, the castle rises up over the small medieval village built against its sides. Its rich past goes back to the 12th century and this feudal fortress, considered impregnable, was conquered however by Simon de Montfort in 1214, during the crusade against the Albigensiens.

During the 100 years war, situated in English territory, the castle was rival to Beynac castle, which remained loyal to the king of France. Both castles were separated by a natural frontier: the Dordogne river. Considered as "the strongest rampart of Perigord" Castelnaud castle was involved in all of the religious battles. The famous Protestant warrior Geoffroy de Vivans was born within its walls. From the 17th century on however, this austere citadel was abandoned in favour of more welcoming dwellings and gradually fell to ruin. It is presently being restored. The visit includes slide shows and explanatory video films as well as reconstitutions of war machinery, an archery room and an arms depot (late 15th century).

Following the Dordogne along the D 53 road, we come to **Fayrac castle**, which is privately owned and not open to visitors. Protected by trees, this beautiful 15th and 16th century building with its watch-turrets was a lookout post for Castelnaud.

A little further on is **Milandes castle**. It was built in 1489 by François de Caumont, lord of Castelnaud and became his main residence. Surrounded by fine terrace gardens, this castle remains linked to the name of Josephine Baker. For many years, she lived here and set up her "village of the world" with her adopted children. The castle apartments can be visited today and contain numerous objects and furniture belonging to the Caumont family and the famous singer.

We can cross the Dordogne by one of two means: either continuing by way of Allas les

Beynac castle reflected in the waters of the Dordogne

Mines or by retracing our steps. The two roads lead us towards a formidable fortress, one of the four baronies of Périgord.

Beynac castle

Built at the top of the cliff, the feudal castle of Beynac proudly overlooks the banks of the Dordogne which reflects its high walls. At its foot hugging the cliff face is the small village which was a port until the 19th century.

We can trace the Beynac family back to the 12th century. The castle was taken by Richard the Lionheart in 1189 and remained in English hands till his death. (He was killed in 1199 during the siege of Châlus in the Limousin region). During the crusade against the Albigensiens, the castle was taken again and Simon de Montfort razed its defences.

The Beynac family remained loyal to the French King during the 100 Years War, and were continually in battle against the Castelnauds. They became Protestant during the Religious wars and finally after many changes of fortune, the unique remaining heiress married the Marquis of Beaumont on the 10th March 1761. The dynasty thus disappeared.

To the south, the castle features an impressive facade extended by a spur-shaped bastion with overhanging towers. The northern section facing the castle was protected by a double wall. The square 13th century dungeon is joined to another 14th century tower by a curtain (wall between two towers) containing loopholes and machicolations. The interior of the castle is be-ing restored but can be visited. In particular, we can see the large "meeting-room of the Perigord states". Here, the nobles of the four baronies met: Beynac and Biron from the South - Bourdeilles and Mareuil from the North. From the curtains and the dungeon, there is a magnificent view of the valley from a different angle. In front of us is the promontory of Domme, and the castles of Marqueyssac, Castelnaud and Fayrac.

If time allows, **Puymartin castle** should be visited. It is on the D. 47 road between Sarlat and les Eyzies. (Described in the 2nd circuit). You can also visit **SAINT Cyprien**, a charming village with its 12th century church and a former 14th and 16th century Augustine abbey. Finally, you should make a detour via **Cadouin**, a former abbey founded in 1115, whose church and cloister are of great interest.

Puymartin castle

La Vézère Circuit

If you have only one day available, you must not miss seeing:

Les Eyzies de Tayac: National Prehistoric Museum
— Open all year every day except Tuesday.
— From 1/03 to 30/11 from 9.30 a.m. to 12 p.m. and 2 p.m. to 6 p.m.
— From 1/12 to 28/02 from 9.30 a.m. to 12 p.m. and 2 p.m. to 5 p.m. Phone: 53.06.97.03

Lascaux II Caves:
— Open from 1/02 to 30/06 from 10 a.m. to 12 p.m. and 2 p.m. to 5 p.m. except Mondays.
— From 1/07 to 31/08 from 9.30 a.m. to 7 p.m. every day.
— From 1/09 to 31/12 from 10 a.m. to 12 p.m. and 2 p.m. to 5 p.m. except Monday.
— In season tickets sold under the archway of the Tourist Office at Montignac from 9 a.m. Groups: Pre and post season only, reservations. Phone: 53.53.44.35

Grotte de Font de Gaume (caves) (Paintings):
— Open all year every day except Tuesday. In peak season, tickets sold at 9 a.m., on site only. Phone: 53.08.00.94.
— From 1/04 to 30/09 from 9 a.m. to 12 p.m. and 2 p.m. to 6 p.m.
— October and March from 10 a.m. to 12 p.m. and 2 p.m. to 5 p.m.
— From 2/11 to 25/02 from 10 a.m. to 12 p.m. and 2 p.m. to 4 p.m.

If you have only 2 or 3 days, we suggest you visit:

Grotte de Combarelles (Engravings):
— Open all year every day except Wednesday. Phone: 53.08.00.94.
— From 1/04 to 31/03 from 10 a.m. to 12 p.m. and 2 p.m. to 4 p.m.
— In peak season, tickets sold at 9 a.m. for the morning 2 p.m. Phone: 53.08.00.94.

Grotte de Rouffignac (Caves) (Caves of the hundred mammouths):
— Palm Sundy to 30/06 from 10 a.m. to 11.30 a.m. and 2 p.m. to 5 p.m.
— From 1/07 to 31/08 from 9 a.m. to 11.30 a.m. and 2 p.m. to 6 p.m.
— From 1/09 to All Saints from 10 a.m. to 11.30 a.m. and 2 p.m. to 5 p.m. Phone: 53.05.41.71.

La Madeleine (Troglodite Fort):
— Open from 1/03 to 30/11 every day except Tuesdays.
— Open from 1/07 to 07/09 every day from 9 a.m. to 12 p.m. and 2 p.m. to 7 p.m. Ph.: 53.53.44.35 - 53.06.92.49.

Prehisto Park:
— Open from 1/03 to 30/04 from 9 a.m. to 12 p.m. and 2 p.m. to 6 p.m.
— From 1/05 to 30/09 from 9 a.m. to 7 p.m.
— From 1/10 to 20/11 from 9 a.m. to 12 p.m. and 2 p.m. to 6 p.m. Ph.: 53.50.73.19 - 53.06.93.48.

La Roque Saint-Christophe (Troglodite fort):
— Open from Easter to 1/11 every day 1/07 to 15/9 from 9.30 a.m. to 6.30 p.m.
— Out of season from 10 a.m. to 12 p.m. and 2 p.m. to 6 p.m. Phone: 53.50.70.45 or 53.07.21.63

Grotte du Grand Roc (Crystal Formations):
— Open every day from 1/03 to 1/11. Phone: 53.06.96.76.
— From 1/07 to 15/09 from 9 a.m. to 6.30 p.m.
— Out of season from 9 a.m. to 12 p.m. and 2 p.m. to 6 p.m.

Proumeyssac Chasm (Crystal Formations):
— Open every day from end of March to all Saint's Day (1 Nov.) from 9 a.m. to 12 p.m. and 2 p.m. to 6.30 p.m.
— Open July-August, all day from 9 a.m. to 7 p.m.
— Easily accessible to elderly and handicapped persons. Phone: 53.07.27.47.
— From 15/1 to 31/11 group visits on reservation.

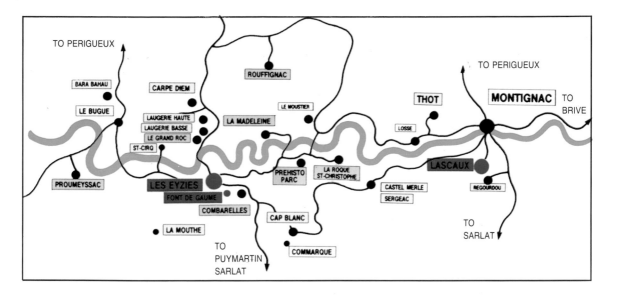

If you have several days available, you will be more than pleased to visit all of the sites we suggest:

Bara Bahau (Engravings):
— Open every day from the Spring holidays (end March) to 30/09 from 9 a.m. to 12 p.m. and 2 p.m. to 6.30 p.m.
— Open July - August from 8.30 a.m. to 7 p.m.
— Easily accessible to elderly and handicapped persons.
— From 15/01 to 31/11 group visits on reservation. Phone: 53.07.28.82.

Sorcerer's Cave (Engravings) (Saint-Cirq):
— Open from 10/06 to 15/09 from 10 a.m. to 6 p.m. every day - except Saturday.
— Out of season from 12 p.m. to 4 p.m. except Saturday.

Laugerie Basse (Field and Museum):
— Open from 1/06 to 30/09 and during the Easter holidays.
— From 9 a.m. to 6 p.m. Phone: 39.19.28.55.

Laugerie Haute (Prehistoric Field):
— Open all year every day except Tuesday. Phone for groups: 53.08.00.94.
— From 1/04 to 30/09 from 9 a.m. to 12 p.m. and 2 p.m. to 6 p.m.
— October and March from 10 a.m. to 12 p.m. and 2 p.m. to 4.30 p.m.
— From 2/11 to 25/02 from 10 a.m. to 12 p.m. and 2 p.m. to 4 p.m.

Carpe Diem (Crystal formations):
— Open from 2/04 to 30/06 from 9 a.m. to 8 p.m.
— Open from 1/07 to 31/08 from 9 a.m. to 12 a.m. (midnight).
— Open from 1/09 to 30/10 from 9 a.m. to 8 p.m. Phone: 53.06.93.63.

Marmites du Ruth:
— Open all year. Phone: 53.50.74.02.

Préhistoric Centre: Le Thot:
— Same hours as Lascaux II - visit with caves. Phone: 53.53.44.35.

Le Regourdou (Préhistoric field):
— Open all year April - June from 9 a.m. to 12 p.m. and 2 p.m. to 6 p.m.
— July and August - permanent visits.
— From 150/09 to 31/03 from 9 a.m. to 12 p.m. - 2 p.m. to 5 p.m. Phone: 53.51.81.23.

Castel Merle Sergeac (Prehistoric shelter):
— Open from Easter to 30/09.
— In July and August from 10 a.m. to 6.30 p.m.
— Out of season, every day (except Wednesday) from 10 a.m. to 12 p.m. and 2 p.m. to 5.30 p.m. Phone: 53.50.77.76.

Abri de Cap Blanc (Sculptures):
— Open from 27/03 to 2/11.
— Open from 1/07 to 31/08 from 10 a.m. to 7 p.m.
— Out of season from 10 a.m. to 12 p.m. and 2 p.m. to 5 p.m. Ph.: 53.59.21.74. Visit by appointment in winter.

Losse Castle:
— Open from 28/6 to 21/09 from 10 a.m. to 12.30 p.m. and 2 p.m. to 6.30 p.m.
— Out of season on request for groups. Phone: 53.50.70.38.

The village of Les Eyzies de Tayac

Around Les Eyzies

From Sarlat, we take the D 47 road towards les Eyzies de Tayac. The road crosses over wooded hills. Several kilometres away, at a bend, we take a right fork which leads up to Puymartin castle, hidden in the woods.

The castle has belonged to the same family for five centuries and was built by the Saint Clairs in the 15th and 16th centuries, then partly restored in the 19th century. Surrounded by a wall of curtains and surmounted by round towers, the interior features 17th and 18th century Renaissance furniture, Aubusson and Beauvais tapestries as well as curious paintings on the woodwork.

Continuing along the road, we will visit the huts or "bories" of Breuil (small stone huts with stone-tiled roofs). We turn right at the crossroads at a garage, then head in the direction of Paradoux. This charming village is about 2 kms away and is surrounded by woods.

The D 47 finally leads us to les **Eyzies de Tayac**, the prehistoric "capital", situated at the junction of the Vézère and Beune rivers at the foot

The representation of prehistoric man, - the work of the sculptor Paul Dardé - welcomes the visitor, awakening his curiosity as to his origins

of impressive cliffs. It is in this decor of caves and shelters, discovered in the second half of the 19th century near the village, that prehistoric science was born. We will now visit all of the sites, starting with les Eyzies, then covering the length of the Vézère valley towards **Montignac**.

Grotte de Font de Gaume - situated on the road to Sarlat, this cave is 125 metres long, an average of 2-3 metres wide and contains several cavities. It has been known to the inhabitants of the area for many years. Its beautiful and numerous polychrome paintings date from the Magdalenian era and were only discovered in 1901. The first paintings appear 50 metres or so after a narrow passage called "Le Rubicon". Inside more than 200 painted or engraved figures representing bison, horses, mammouths, deer, oxen, rhinoceros etc., have been counted. In season, the queue is quite long, but this should not discourage you from seeing these admirable frescos.

The troglodite village on the site of La Madeleine

La Grotte des Combarelles is situated next to Font de Gaume and was discovered several days before the latter. It consists of a 250 metre long corridor with more than 300 mural paintings of horses, bison, mammouths as well as paintings of humans. These works date from the mid-Magdalenian era and have greatly contributed to the recognition of prehistoric mural art.

At **les Eyzies**, you must see the National Prehistoric museum, situated in the former medieval castle overlooking the village. Those unfamiliar with the prehistoric era will learn much from the clear and comprehensive presentation of the numerous objects. Heading towards Manaurie through the small valley named "Les Gorges d'Enfer", we will visit the speleology museum.

The **Grotte du Grand Roc** is next on our itinerary. You will discover its magnificent formations - a veritable tapestry of stalactites and stalagmites of great variety and form which seemingly defies the law of gravity in some places. (The visit lasts approx. 30 mins.).

On the site of **Laugerie Basse**, numerous objects and tools dating from the Magdalenian to the Azilian age (from 12 000 to 8 000 B.C.) have been discovered. Some of the objects are exhibited in a small museum. At **Laugerie Haute**, the prehistoric shelter is 200 metres long and studies of its different strata have enabled us to gain knowledge of the eras from the Gravetian to the Magdalenian and in particular, the Solutrian.

After **Manaurie**, we will visit the cave of **Carpe Diem** with its crystal formations. It contains a 180 metre long corridor of numerous stalactites and stalagmites. On the road to **Bugue**, near the small village of **Saint-Cirq**, the "Grotte du Sorcier", (sorcerer's cave), features numerous engravings of the Magdalenian era and in particular, engravings of three humans, of which the sorcerer is one of the finest examples of mural art. (The visit lasts approximately 20 minutes).

Bara Bahau cave, situated in the hill overlooking Bugue is interesting from a geological aspect due to the excavations which reveal the different strata. In particular however, it features a number of engravings of great interest (horses, bison, bears etc.) drawn with flint and dating from the Upper Perigordian period. (The visit lasts approximately 35 minutes).

A few kilometres away from **Bugue**, we should visit **Proumeyssac** chasm hidden in the forest. To facilitate access, a tunnel leads to the interior of the chasm. A sound and light show highlights the beauty of this cupola-shaped "cathedral of crystal". It is the only chasm in the Perigord region and features in particular, petrified fountains. (Duration of the visit: approx. 35 mins.).

Returning towards **les Eyzies**, another cave, La Grotte de la **Mouthe**, discovered in 1894, fea-

The interior of Proumeyssac Chasm

tures engravings of bison, horses, mammouths etc.

From les Eyzies to Montignac

Heading towards Montignac, we arrive at the site of **La Madeleine**, which has given its name to a period of the Upper Paleolithic age: The Magdalenian era. Prehistoric man lived in this region from 12 000 to 8 000 B.C. and since 1863, excavations have revealed much about their way of life. Above the site, we will visit troglodyte dwellings which have been occupied since the Middle Ages, and the ruins of the castle overlooking the Vézère valley.

A few kilometres away, in the green and wooded surrondings of a small valley, the **Prehistoric Park** displays reconstructions of the daily life of the first Neanderthal hunters.

Reconstruction of a Prehistoric hunting scene in the Prehistoric Park

The impressive site of la Roque St Christophe with its enormous cliff, long ago occupied by a citadel and a troglodite fort

The site of **La Roque Saint-Christophe** was occupied by prehistoric men in the Mousterian epoch. (50 000 B.C.). Successive civilisations followed, inhabiting a fort and a troglodyte citadel built on this impressive cliff 900 metres long and 80 metres high.

On the right bank of the Vézère, excavations made on the site of **Moustier** have revealed a Neanderthal skeleton and numerous tools. These have enabled us to characterise an epoch of the Mid-Paleolithic age - the Mousterian epoch.

The **Grotte de Rouffignac** or "Cro de Granville" cave stretches out over more than 8 kms of underground galleries which the visitor can see from a small electric train. The existence of the cave has been known since the 16th century and its remarkable paintings and engravings were discovered in 1956. They date from the late Magdalenian era and depict rhinosceros, bison, horses, ibex, and particularly mammouths, which explains the name, "Cave of the Hundred Mammouths".

Around Montignac

The ticket that you buy to visit the replica of **Lascaux** prehistoric caves is also valid for Thot, the prehistoric art centre whose numerous features, (films, models, animal park etc.) will enable you to gain a better knowledge of the prehistoric era.

Near **Montignac**, Losse castle is built on the cliff overlooking the Vézère river. This 16th century building features machicolations and slop-

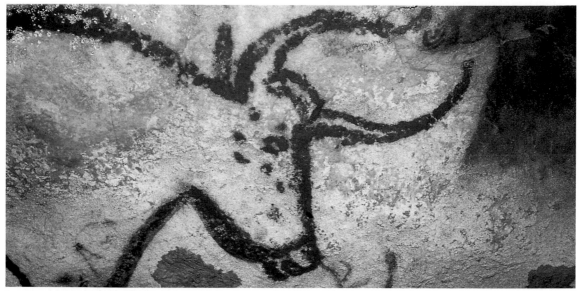

Lascaux: Bulls heads and horses heads in the great gallery

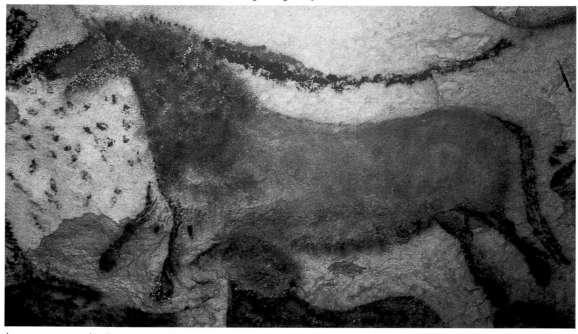

Lascaux caves: in the great gallery, red horse and small brown horses

ing roofs with a round tower topped by a watch-turret. We can visit the interior which contains sumptuous furnishings.

Montignac was the former fief of the Perigord counts but the village became renowned world-wide with the discovery of Lascaux caves on the 14th September 1940, by four youths who were looking for their dog lost in a hole. One of the finest sites of polychrome paintings was thus revealed.

Unfortunately, the destruction of these immense frescos by external pollution has necessitated its closure to the public. However, a perfect facsimile of the Bull gallery and the axial cavity was opened several years ago. It is an exact replica of the magnificent mural paintings.

Near **Lascaux**, the prehistoric site of Régourdou, situated on a hill overlooking **Montignac** was discovered in March 1954. It has revealed animal burial grounds - amongst them a large

Losse Castle overlooking the Vézère river

number of brown bears, as well as the remains of a Neanderthal man 70 000 years old.

From Montignac, we can continue towards **les Eyzies** along the Vézère valley. We pass in front of Losse and Belcaire castles which are reflected in the waters of the Dordogne, then through the small village of **Saint-Leon-sur-Vézère**. At Sergeac, we can visit the prehistoric site of Castel Merle with its shelters: Reverdit, Labattut and La Souquette. In the latter, we can see a cross-section which reveals the different layers from the early Paleolithic era to the present day.

Descending towards Sireuil, we should visit the prehistoric sculptures of Cap Blanc - horse frescos and Magdalenian deers. Opposite the site, in the beautiful Beune valley, are the ruins of the imposing Commarque castle, built in the 12th and 13th centuries.

Besides these two circuits, you must visit the country house of Monpazier, built by Edward 1st of England, Villefranche de Perigord with is beautiful covered market, and in particular, Biron castle.